First World War
and Army of Occupation
War Diary
France, Belgium and Germany

1 DIVISION
2 Infantry Brigade
Headquarters
1 January 1919 - 30 July 1919

WO95/1268/2

The Naval & Military Press Ltd
www.nmarchive.com
Published in association with The National Archives

Published by

The Naval & Military Press Ltd

Unit 10 Ridgewood Industrial Park,
Uckfield, East Sussex,
TN22 5QE England
Tel: +44 (0) 1825 749494

www.naval-military-press.com
www.nmarchive.com

This diary has been reprinted in facsimile from the original. Any imperfections are inevitably reproduced and the quality may fall short of modern type and cartographic standards.

© Crown Copyright
Images reproduced by permission of The National Archives, London, England, 2015.

Contents

Document type	Place/Title	Date From	Date To
Miscellaneous	March Table To Accompany 2nd Infantry Brigade Order No.251		
Operation(al) Order(s)	2nd Infantry Brigade Order No.250	08/12/1918	08/12/1918
Miscellaneous	March Table To Accompany 2nd Infantry Brigade Order No. 250		
Operation(al) Order(s)	2nd Infantry Brigade Order No.249	06/12/1918	06/12/1918
Operation(al) Order(s)	2nd Infantry Brigade Order No.248	01/12/1918	01/12/1918
Miscellaneous	March Table For 2nd December to Accompany 2nd Infantry Brigade Order No.248		
Miscellaneous	Addendum To March Table For 3rd December In With 2nd Infantry Brigade Order No.248	03/12/1918	03/12/1918
Miscellaneous	March Table For 3rd December in Accordance With 2nd Infantry Brigade Order No.248	02/12/1918	02/12/1918
War Diary	Duisdorf	01/01/1919	31/01/1919
Miscellaneous	Appendix I		
War Diary	Messdorf	01/03/1919	28/03/1919
Miscellaneous	Headquarters Western Division	06/04/1919	06/04/1919
War Diary		06/03/1919	31/03/1919
Miscellaneous	Appendix II		
Miscellaneous	Message Form		
Miscellaneous	Appendix I		
Operation(al) Order(s)	2nd Infantry Brigade Order No.262	05/03/1919	05/03/1919
Miscellaneous	Brigade Administrative Instructions No.1. in Connection with the Arrival of Young Soldiers Battns.	04/03/1919	04/03/1919
Operation(al) Order(s)	2nd Infantry Brigade Order No.263	30/03/1919	30/03/1919
Miscellaneous	Appendix IV		
Miscellaneous	Defence Of Bonn 2nd Infantry Brigade Instructions No.1		
Miscellaneous	Issued Through No.3 Signal Section at 17.00 Hours 12th March 1919		
Miscellaneous	Appendix II to 2nd Infantry Brigade Instruction No.1		
Miscellaneous	Appendix III to 2nd Infantry Brigade Instruction No.1		
Miscellaneous	Addendum No.1 To 3rd Infantry Brigade Administrative Instructions No.1	05/03/1919	05/03/1919
Miscellaneous	Defence Of Bonn 2nd Infantry Brigade Instructions No.2	20/03/1919	20/03/1919
Miscellaneous	Defence Of Bonn 2nd Infantry Brigade Instructions No.3	27/03/1919	27/03/1919
Miscellaneous	Reference Map Of Bonn 1/10,000, Appendix 1 Of 2nd Infantry Brigade Instruction No.1	27/03/1919	27/03/1919
Heading	War Diary of 2nd Western Infantry Brigade (formerly-2nd Infantry Brigade) From 1st April, 1919 To 30th April, 1919		
War Diary		10/04/1919	30/04/1919
Heading	War Diary of 2nd Western Infantry Brigade From 1st May 1919 To 31st May, 1919		
War Diary	Medinghoven	01/05/1919	16/05/1919
Heading	War Diary of 2nd Western Infantry Brigade Headquarters, From 1st June, 1919 To 30th June, 1919		
War Diary	Medinghoven	01/06/1919	19/06/1919

War Diary	Bonn	20/06/1919	29/06/1919
War Diary	Medinghoven	30/06/1919	30/06/1919
Heading	War Diary of 2nd Western Infantry Brigade Headquarters. From 1st July, 1919-To 31st July, 1919		
War Diary	Medinghoven	07/07/1919	30/07/1919

MARCH TABLE TO ACCOMPANY 2ND INFANTRY BRIGADE ORDER No.251.

Serial.	Unit.	From	To	Starting Point.	Pass at	Route.	Remarks.
1	R.Sussex.	SINSIN	HOTTON	Rd.fork MARCHE 3.D.23.38.	1015	HEURE NOISEUX DEULIN.	Via 2nd Class road SINSIN to HEURE.
2	Northamptons.	-do-	-do-	-do-	1022	-do-	
3	2nd T.M.Bty.	-do-	-do-	-do-	1029	-do-	Via SINSIN to S.F.
4	2nd.I.R.R.C.	HAVERSIN.	MELREUX.	31 Km.stone on HAVERSIN - NETTINNE Rd.	0928	NETTINNE HEURE NOISEUX DEULIN	To pass HEURE road fork 3.D. 60.58 in rear of Serial 3 at 1116.
5	1st Bn.M.G.C.	HAID.	FRONVILLE & MOIVILLE.	-do-	0934	-do-	
6	2nd Bde.H.Qrs.	CHAU.de la FONTAINE.	DEULIN.	-do-	0949	-do-	
7	409 Fd.Coy.RE.	HAVERSIN.	HOTTON.	-do-	1000	-do-	
8	No.3 Coy.Train.	-do-	MELREUX.	-do-	1005	-do-	
9	No.2 Fd.Amb.	-do-	DEULIN.	-do-	1007	-do-	
10.	2nd Line Trans- port of R.Sussex and North'n R. & supply wagons for whole Group.	SINSIN.	-	As for Serial 1.	1215		Joins column at HEURE road fork 3.D.60.58. in rear of Serial 9 at 1200.
11	2nd Line Trans- port of K.R.R.C. & 1st Bn.M.G.C.	HAVERSIN.	-	As for Serial 4.	1017		Not to pass HEURE road fork 3.D.60.58 till Serial No.10 is clear.

SECRET.   Copy No. 20

2ND INFANTRY BRIGADE ORDER NO.250.

8th December, 1918.

Ref. Map, MARCHE, 1/100,000.

1.   The Support Group will continue the march on the 9th December in accordance with the march table overleaf.

2.   Billeting parties will meet representatives of Brigade Hd.Qrs. as under :-

1st Bn.M.G.Corps.	At CHURCH, HAID, at 0730 hrs.
2nd K.R.R.Corps.) 409th Fd.Coy.,R.E.) No.3 Coy.Train.) No.2 Fd.Ambulance.)	At CHURCH, HAVERSIN, at 0740 hrs.
2nd T.M.Bty.	At X Roads ½ mile West of 1st S in SINSIN, at 36 Km. stone, at 0755 hrs.
2nd R.Sussex.) 1st Northamptons.)	At CHURCH, SINSIN, at 0800 hrs.

3.   2nd Line Transport of Infantry Units will march brigaded under orders of B.T.O. Each Battalion will detail one Platoon to march in rear of its 2nd Line Transport, and C.O., 2nd K.R.R.Corps will detail one Platoon to march in rear of remaining transport.

4.   Lorries will rendezvous at the road fork ¾ mile E. of CHEVETOGNE ABBEY at 0930 hrs, and will proceed brigaded under 2/Lieut.S.JOHNSON.

5.   Refilling point for 9th MONT-GAUTHIER.

6.   ACKNOWLEDGE.

thro' No.3 Sig.Sect.
Issued at 1155 hrs.

Captain, Brigade Major,
2nd Infantry Brigade.

Copies to :-
1. R.Sussex.
2. Northamptons.
3. K.R.R.Corps.
4. T.M.Battery.
5. 409th Fd.Coy.,R.E.
6. No.2 Fd.Amb.
7. No.3 Coy.,1st Div. Train.
8. 1st Bn.M.G.Corps.
9. 25th Bde.R.F.A. (For inf.)
10. Advanced Group.
11. Div.Group.
12. Staff Capt.
13. Bde.Signal Offr.
14. B.T.O.
15. Bde.Supply Offr.
16 & 17. 1st Division.
18. A.D.M.S.
19. A.P.M.
20 & 21. War Diary.
22. File.

MARCH TABLE TO ACCOMPANY 2ND INFANTRY BRIGADE ORDER NO.250.

No.	Unit.	From	To	Starting Point.	Pass at	Route.	Remarks.
1	1st North'n R.	CHEVETOGNE ABBEY.	SINSIN.	Rd. junct. ½ mile E. of CHEVETOGNE ABBEY.	1036.		
2	2nd R.Sussex.	MONTGAUTHIER	-do-	-do-	1036		
3	2nd Bde.H.Q.	CHAU.ROYAL de JAMBJOUL.	CHAU. de la FONTAINE.	-do-	1042		
4	2nd T.M.B.	JAMBJOUL	SINSIN	-do-	1043		
5	2nd K.R.R.C.	CLERGNON.	HAVERSIN.	-do-	1044		
6	No.2 Fd.Amb.	JAMBLINNE.	-do-	-do-	1100		
7	409 Fd.Coy.RE.	BRIQUEMONT.	The CHURCH, LALOUX.	-do-	1008	FRANDEUX NAVAUGLE.	Join column at road fork 4.0. 17.76. at 1139 in rear of No.6.
8	No.3 Coy Train.	CLERGNON.		As for Ser.l.	1110		
9	2nd Line Transport.	-		-do-	1112		
10	1st En.M.G.Corps.	HOUYET.	HAID.	Starting Point as ordered by Div.Group Commdr.	0900		Pass Starting Point for Serial No.1 at about 1130 hrs.

SECRET.
Copy No. 18

2ND INFANTRY BRIGADE ORDER NO.249.

6th December, 1918.

Ref. Map, MARCHE, 1/100,000.

1. The following moves will take place to-morrow, 7th inst:-

No.	Unit.	From	To	Taking over from	Start. Point.	Pass at	Remarks.
1	R.Sussex.	WANLIN.	MONT-GAUTHIER.	6th Welsh Regt.	3 Km. stone on CIERGNON-ROCHEFORT RD.	1100	via CIERGNON to Starting Point.
2	North'n Regt.	VILLERS-sur-LESSE.	CHEVETOGNE ABBEY.	1st Camerons.	-do-	1106	
3	2nd Line Transport of both Battns.	-	-	-	-do-	1112	March under orders of Major E.D.GOULD, M.C., 1st North'n R.

ROUTE. Main road through BOIS de MONT-GAUTHIER, for all Units.

2. Billeting parties will report at the H.Q. of Battalions of Advanced Group, at 0830 hours to take over accommodation.
   Guides will meet incoming Battalions at the 1 Km. stone (MARCHE 4.B.75.50) under Battalion arrangements.

3. Each Battalion will detail one Platoon to march in rear of its own 2nd Line Transport, to assist with drag ropes in case of necessity.

4. Completion of move will be at once reported to Brigade Headquarters.

5. ACKNOWLEDGE.

Captain, Brigade Major,
2nd Infantry Brigade.

Issued at 1630 hrs.
Copies to :-
1. R.Sussex.
2. Northamptons.
3. K.R.R.Corps.
4. T.M.Battery.
5. 409th Fd.Coy.,R.E.
6. No.2 Fd.Amb.
7. No.3 Coy., 1st Div.Train.
8. 25th Bde.R.F.A.
9. Advanced Group.
10. Staff Capt.
11. Bde.Signal Offr.
12. B.T.O.
13. Bde. Supply Offr.
14 & 15. 1st Division.
16. A.D.M.S.
17. A.P.M.
18 & 19. War Diary.
20. File.

SECRET.   Copy No. 17

2ND INFANTRY BRIGADE ORDER NO.248.

Ref. Maps, NAMUR, 1/100,000.   1st December, 1918.
          MARCHE, 1/100,000.

1. The 1st Division will be concentrated East of the MEUSE by December 3rd.

2. The Group will continue the march to-morrow, 2nd inst., in accordance with the march table overleaf.
   The march table for 3rd instant will be forwarded later.

3. Billeting arrangements will be notified separately.

4. 2nd Line Transport of Infantry Units will march Brigaded under the orders of the Brigade Transport Officer.

5. O.C., 1st Northamptonshire Regt. will detail one Coy. as baggage guard on the 2nd, and O.C., 2nd K.R.R.Corps a similar guard on the 3rd. These Companies will march in rear of 2nd Line Transport and will be available with drag-ropes in case of emergency.

6. Lorries will rendezvous daily at the Brigade Starting Point at 0900 hours and will proceed Brigaded under orders of 2/Lieut. S. JOHNSON.

7. Time and place of refilling will be notified later.

8. The Divisional Band will be at DINANT BRIDGE and will play Battalions across to their Regimental Marches.

9. ACKNOWLEDGE.

                                            Captain, Brigade Major,
                                            2nd Infantry Brigade.

Issued at 1915 hrs.

Copies to :-
1. R.Sussex.   10. Bde.Supply Offr.
2. Northamptons.   11. No.3 Coy., 1st Div. Train.
3. K.R.R.C.   12. 25th Bde.R.F.A.
4. T.M.Bty.   13 & 14. 1st Division.
5. 409th Fd.Coy.,R.E.   15. A.D.M.S.
6. No.2 Fd.Amb.   16. A.P.M.
7. Staff Captain.   17 & 18. War Diary.
8. Bde.Signal Offr.   19. File.
9. B.T.O.

MARCH TABLE FOR 2nd DECEMBER.
TO ACCOMPANY 2ND INFANTRY BRIGADE ORDER NO.248.

Serial No.	Unit.	From	To.	Sub.Start. Point.	Pass at.	Bde.Start. Point.	Pass at.	Remarks.
1	2nd K.R.R.C.	CHESTRUVIN.	FOY N'DAME.	38 Kr.stone on ONHAYE-DINANT RD. (NAMUR 3.K.70.03)	1035	Rd.fork N. of DINANT BRIDGE. 3.K.88.13.	1103.	
2	2nd R.Sussex.	ONHAYE.	CELLES.	-do-	1041	-do-	1109	
3	2nd T.M.Bty.	WEILLEN.	SOINNE.	-do-	1047	-do-	1115	
4	2nd Bde.H.Q.	CHAT. de MON-TAIGLE.	MIRANDA CHATEAU (4.L.90.66)	Rd.fork B.K. 60.28. immediately S. of V in BOUVIGNES.	1030	-do-	1116	
5	1st North'n Regt.	SOMMIERE.	MIRANDA CHATEAU	-do-	1031	-do-	1117	
6	409 Fd.Coy.RE.	ROSTENNE.	LAVYS.	-do-	1037	-do-	1123	
7	25 Bde.R.F.A.	WEILLEN.	VEVE & GENDRON.	As for Serial No.1.	1110	-do-	1128	Tail to be clear of DINANT BRIDGE by 1150.
8. ✱	2nd Line Transport of Inf. Units.			(KRRC. } As for (Sussex.} Ser.1. (North'n } As for (Regt. } Ser.4.		-do-	1200	
9.	No.3 Coy Train.	ONHAYE.	BOISELIES.	As for Serial No.1.	1136	-do-	1204	
10.	No.2 Fd.Amb.	WEILLEN.	-do-	-do-	1141	-do-	1209.	

✱ Rendezvous at Brigade Starting Point at 1150. Order of march from Starting Point - 2nd K.R.R.C.; 2nd R.Sussex. 1st Northamptons.
ROUTE. DINANT - CELLES ROAD.

ADDENDUM TO MARCH TABLE FOR 3RD DECEMBER.
IN *accordance* WITH 2ND INFANTRY BRIGADE ORDER NO.248.

Serial No.	Unit.	Destination.
1	2nd R.Sussex.	WANLIN.
2	1st Northamptons.	VILLERS-sur-LESSE.
3	2nd Bde.H.Qrs.	WANLIN.
4	2nd T.M.Battery.	JAMBJOUL
5	2nd K.R.R.Corps.	CIERGNON.
6	409th Field Coy.,R.E.	BRIQUEMONT.
7	25th Brigade,R.F.A.	LALOUX and FRANIEUX.
8.	No.3 Coy. Train.	CIERGNON.
9.	No.2 Field Ambulance.	JAMBLINNE.

through No.3 Sig.Sect
Issued at 0700 hrs. 3/12/18.

[signature]
Captain, Brigade Major,
2nd Infantry Brigade.

MARCH TABLE FOR 3RD DECEMBER.
IN ACCORDANCE WITH 2ND INFANTRY BRIGADE ORDER NO.248.

Serial No.	Unit.	From.	Starting Point.	Pass at	Remarks.
1	2nd R.Sussex.	CELLES.	10 Km. stone on CELLES - CIERGNON RD. MARCHE 4.A.30.56.	1005	Route from Starting Point via CIERGNON. Destination of Units will be notified later. Artillery from VEVE via CELLES to Starting Point. Not to enter village till Serial 5 is clear. Artillery from GENDRON via LAVYS and SOINNE to Starting Point. Not to enter LAVYS till Serial No.6 is clear.
2	1st North'n R.	MIRANDA CHATEAU.	-do-	1011	
3	2nd Inf.Bde.H.Q.	-do-	-do-	1017	
4	2nd T.M.Bty.	SOINNE	-do-	1018	
5	2nd K.R.R.C.	FOY N'DAME.	-do-	1019	
6	409 Fd.Coy.R.E.	LAVYS.	-do-	1025	
7	25th Bde.R.F.A.	VEVE & GENDRON.	-do-	1030	
8	2nd Line Transport of Inf. Units.		-do-	1100	
9	No.3 Coy. Train.	NOISELLES.	-do-	1104	
10	No.2 Fd.Amb.	-do-	-do-	1109	

[signature]
Captain, Brigade Major,
2nd Infantry Brigade.

Issued at 1025 hrs. 2/12/18.

Army Form C. 2118

HQ 2 Infy Bde

WAR DIARY
or
INTELLIGENCE SUMMARY
(Erase heading not required.)

Instructions regarding War Diaries and Intelligence Summaries are contained in F. S. Regs., Part II and the Staff Manual respectively. Title Pages will be prepared in manuscript.

Place	Date	Hour	Summary of Events and Information	Remarks and references to Appendices
DUISDORF	January 1st to 31st		No events of importance have occurred during the month. Military, Educational and Recreational Training continued on approved lines. Association Football Competitions commenced towards the middle of the month, but were delayed by frost and snow. Miniature Rifle Ranges were completed by all units, and a Brigade 400 yards Range was taken in hand. Units were located as under :- 2nd Infantry Brigade Headquarters......Medinghoven Chateau. 2nd Royal Sussex..................Witterschlick. 1st Northamptonshire Regiment.....Duisdorf. 2nd K.R.R.C......................Duisdorf. 2nd K.R.R.C......................Alfter. 2nd T. M. Battery................Messdorf. 3rd February, 1919. Brigadier General, Commanding 2nd Infantry Brigade.	

Army Form C. 2118

Vol 54

WAR DIARY
or
INTELLIGENCE SUMMARY
(Erase heading not required.)

Instructions regarding War Diaries and Intelligence Summaries are contained in F.S. Regs., Part II. and the Staff Manual respectively. Title Pages will be prepared in manuscript.

Place	Date	Hour	Summary of Events and Information	Remarks and references to Appendices
	February.		The Brigade Area remained unchanged during the Month.	
			Training, chiefly of Recreational and Educational nature, continued without intermission. Brigade competitions were organised in the following:-	Appendix I

			Inter-Company Association Football,
			    Inter-Unit Association Football,
			    Cross Country Run.
			    Tug-o-War,
			    Boxing.	

			A list of the winners is annexed.	
			The 1st Division also held competitions in the above events, the finals being played on the 27th February.	
			During the month each Battalion was inspected on ceremonial parade on the 20th, 21st and 24th, by Brigadier General G.C.Kelly, G.S.O., the usual opportunity being given for stating grievances, if any, (Kings Regulations & Orders, para. 128). No grievances were brought forward.	
			Capt. A.W.Ferguson, Royal Scottish Fusiliers, Staff Captain, 2nd Infantry Brigade, was appointed Brigade Major 6th Infantry Brigade on 31st January 1919 (authority dated 24th January 1919), and his place was taken by Capt. G.B.Bruce, M.C. West Riding Regiment.	
	3rd March 1919.			

                                                Brigadier General,
                                       Commanding 2nd Infantry Brigade.

APPENDIX I

Inter-Company Association Football:-

"A" Team....No.2 Field Ambulance.
"B" Team...."B" Coy, 1st Northamptonshire Regt.

Inter-Unit Association Football:-

1st Northamptonshire Regiment.

Cross Country Run.-

1. L/Cpl. Edwards...............2nd Royal Sussex.
2. Lieut. Carrick...............1st Northamptonshire Regt.
3. Pte. Grover, W.E.............2nd Royal Sussex.

4. Bandsman Makinson, J.........2nd K.R.R.C.
5. L/Cpl. Harding, F.G..........1st Northamptonshire Regt.
6. 2nd Lieut: Scolding, H.V....   Do.
~~7. Pte. Reed, G.~~
7. L/Cpl Woolley, H.W...........2nd Royal Sussex.
8. Pte. Reed, G................   Do.
9. Pte. Stevens, H.............   Do.
10. Sgt. Done, H.A..............2nd K.R.R.C.
11. Pte. Seymour A..............2nd Royal Sussex
12. Sgt. Lewis, L...............   Do.

Tug-o-War

Leight Weight.......No.2 Field Ambulance,

Heavy Weight........1st Northamptonshire Regt.

Boxing.

Bantams......Pte. Blades..........2nd Royal Sussex.
Feather......Rfn. French..........2nd K.R.R.C.
Light.......Pte. Murphy..........2nd K.R.R.C. attd 2nd T.M.B
Welter......Pte.Middlemiss.......1st Northamptons
Middle......L/Cpl Pilcher........1st Northamptons
Heavy.......C.Q.M.S.Moles........2nd Royal Sussex.

WAR DIARY
or
INTELLIGENCE SUMMARY
(Erase heading not required.)

Army Form C. 2118.

30th Armd Div. 1919 __ 2nd Trench Mortar Battery

Place	Date	Hour	Summary of Events and Information	Remarks and references to Appendices
Muisdorf	1/13		Commenced course for 18 OR's & 1 Subaltern from Right Brench Mortar of 6 ORs from 2nd Lincolns Regt. & 6 ORs from 19 Northamptonshire Regt. Both from 2nd RMFC.	
			Xc course consist of description of K Mortar, Bombs & fuzes, Charge etc, Mortar drill Emplacement, Care of ammunition, laying, also use of Mortars for Air-craft. Each Educational & Recreational training was carried out, also two hours Mortars according to programme.	
	14		Class having dispersed, remainder of Battery Chancery.	
	15		Routs March	
	16/17		Church Annee	
	/23		The Battery carried out daily training including Musketry Exercises, Arms Drill, P.T & Educational training as per programme.	
	23/28		Deflection of 50% owing to demobilization. Educational carried out.	

CONFIDENTIAL

Headquarters　　　　　　　　　　　　　2nd. Bde. No. 420/10

　　Western Division.

Herewith War Diaries for March 1919.

6th April, 1919.　　　　　　　　　　　　　Brigadier General,
　　　　　　　　　　　　　　　　　Commanding 2nd Infantry Brigade.

Army Form C. 2118.

WAR DIARY
or
INTELLIGENCE SUMMARY.
(Erase heading not required.)

Instructions regarding War Diaries and Intelligence Summaries are contained in F.S. Regs., Part II. and the Staff Manual respectively. Title pages will be prepared in manuscript.

Place	Date	Hour	Summary of Events and Information	Remarks and references to Appendices
	MARCH		During the month the 2nd Infantry Brigade was reformed as under:-	
	6th		The 52nd Battalion the Welch Regiment replaced the 1st Battalion the Northamptonshire (48th) Regiment at DUISDORF, the relieved Battalion moving to LENGSDORF where it wasted to cadre strength.	See Appendix I.
	17th		Colonel (T/Brigadier General) T.O.Marden, C.B., C.M.G., assumed command of the 2nd Infantry Brigade vice Bt. Lieut-Colonel (T/Brigadier General) G.C.Kelly, D.S.O., who relinquished his appointment.	
	25th		The 52nd Battalion the South Wales Borderers replaced the 2nd Battalion the Royal Sussex (35th) Regiment at WITTERSCHLICK, the latter Battalion moving to ODEKOVEN and GIELSDORF to waste to cadre strength.	See Appendix II.
	26th		The 53rd Battalion The Welch Regiment replaced the 2nd Battalion The King's Royal Rifle Corps (60th Rifles) at ALFTER, the Rifles proceeding to DRANSDORF and MESSDORF to waste to a cadre.	
	31st		The 52nd Battalion the South Wales Borderers moved to ARLOFF and KIRSPENICH on transfer to the 3rd Infantry Brigade.	
			The 2nd Battalion The King's Royal Rifle Corps took over billets at WITTERSCHLICK from the 52nd Battalion The South Wales Borderers, clearing DRANSDORF, which then fell into the X Corps Area.	
			The 51st Battalion The Welch Regiment moved from FLAMERSHEIM to MECKENHEIM coming on arrival under the 2nd Infantry Brigade.	See Appendix III.
			On conclusion of the above moves and reliefs, the 2nd Infantry Brigade was constituted as under:-	

Army Form C. 2118.

WAR DIARY
or
INTELLIGENCE SUMMARY.
(Erase heading not required.)

Instructions regarding War Diaries and Intelligence Summaries are contained in F. S. Regs., Part II. and the Staff Manual respectively. Title pages will be prepared in manuscript.

Place	Date	Hour	Summary of Events and Information	Remarks and references to Appendices

Unit   Location

The 2nd Infantry Brigade H.Q.   MEDINGHOVEN BERG.
The 51st Battn. The Welch Regiment   MECKENHEIM.
The 52nd Battn. The Welch Regiment   DUISDORF.
The 53rd Battn. The Welch Regiment   ALFTER.
The 2nd Light Trench Mortar Battery   MESSDORF.
Cadre (The 2nd Royal Sussex Regiment.   ODEKOVEN and GIELSDORF.
       (The 1st Battn. The Northamptonshire Regt.   LENGSDORF.
Battalions.(The 2nd Battn The King's Royal Rifle Corps   WITTERSCHLICK.

During the month in furtherance of 1st Division letter No. G. 707/4 of 24th February 1919, plans were formulated for the defence of BONN in the event of riots or of trouble on the perimeter. The Brigade Group in either of these events would be increased by:-

        1 Section of 18 pounders (104 Brigade Royal Field Artillery)
        "D" Company, the 1st Battalion, Machine Gun Corps.
        No. 2 Field Ambulance.

The plans made are shown in detail in 2nd Infantry Brigade Instructions Nos 1 to 3 and 2nd Infantry Brigade No. G.10/15 of 27th March 1919.

The 2nd Infantry Brigade Administrative Area was increased during the month by the addition of LENGSDORF and IPPENDORF. DRANSDORF, however, was handed over to the X Corps.

See Appendix IV.

/Training,

Army Form C. 2118.

WAR DIARY
or
INTELLIGENCE SUMMARY.
(Erase heading not required.)

Place	Date	Hour	Summary of Events and Information	Remarks and references to Appendices
			Training, both Military Educational and Recreational, continued throughout the month so far as was compatible with the moves and reliefs of units.	
			[signature] Brigadier General, Commanding 2nd Infantry Brigade.	

APPENDIX II

MESSAGE FORM. Series No. of Message

Army Form C 2128 (pads of 100).

TO 2nd Royal Sussex

FROM & place 2nd Inf. Bde.

Originator's Number	Day of Month	In reply to Number
H.841	23/3	

Battalion will vacate WITTERSCHLICK tomorrow 24th and take billets already arranged for in ODEKOVEN and GIELSDORF AAA Report completion of move AAA Acknowledge. AAA Addsd 2nd Royal Sussex reptd 2nd K.R.R.C. 52nd Welch Regt. 2nd T.M.B. No.2 Field Amb. 3 Coy. Train, Western Div: A.D.M.S. A.P.M. 2nd Inf. Bde. Supply Officer.

Captain, Brigade Major

MESSAGE FORM. Series No. of Message _____

CALL	In v—	Reed. At ____ By ____ Sent	Army Form C 2128 (pads of 100).
	Out __ v	At ____ By ____	Date Stamp.

PREAMBLE _____

M.M. Offices { Delivery _____ v
{ Origin _____

PREFIX _____ Words _____

TO

2nd K.R.R.C.

FROM & place: 2nd Inf. Bde

Originator's Number	Day of Month	In reply to Number
H. 848	24/3	

Battalion will vacate ALFTER tomorrow 25th and will take billets already arranged for in DRANSDORF and MESSDORF AAA Report completion of move AAA Acknowledge AAA Addsd 2nd K.R.R.C. Reptd 2nd R. Sussex, 52nd Welch 2nd T.M.B. No, 2 Field Amb: 3 Coy Train: Western Div: A.D.M.S. A.P.M. 2nd Inf. Bde Supply Officer.

TIME OF ORIGIN

TIME OF HANDING IN (For Signal use only).

Originator's Signature (Not Telegraphed)

Captain, Bde, Major,

APPENDIX I

SECRET   Copy No. 16

2nd INFANTRY BRIGADE ORDER No. 362.

5th March 1919.

Ref. Map - EUSKIRCHEN 10/100,000

1. The 52nd Battalion Welch Regiment entrained at DUNKIRK on the 4th instant, and will detrain at DUISDORF at an early date in relief of the 1st Battalion The Northamptonshire Regiment.

2. (a) The 52nd Battalion Welch Regiment on arrival will be accommodated at DUISDORF with 1 Company at LESSENICH.

    (b) The 1st Battalion The Northamptonshire Regiment less transport will vacate their present billets at DUISDORF and move to LENGSDORF on the 6th instant; move to be completed by 14.00 hours.

    Any additional transport required for this move will be applied for by 16.00 hours on the 5th instant.

3. The 1st Battalion The Northamptonshire Regiment will detail 1 Officer and 1 N.C.O. from Headquarters, 1 Officer per Company, and 1 N.C.O. per platoon, to meet the incoming unit, and act as guide to billets. The Headquarter party, and 1 N.C.O. per Company, will remain with the incoming unit for 24 hours, or longer if desired, and will then rejoin their Battalion at LENGSDORF.

    The rear party provided for in this paragraph is in substitution for that provided for in paragraph 3 of 2nd Infantry Brigade Instructions No.1 of 4th March.

4. Completion of the move ordered in para. 2, sub-para. (b), and location of new Battalion Headquarters, will be reported to 2nd Infantry Brigade Headquarters by 18.00 hours 6th instant.

5. ACKNOWLEDGE.

                                               Captain, Brigade Major,
                                               2nd Infantry Brigade.

Issued through No.3 Signal Section at 17.00 hours.

Copies to :-
1. 2nd Royal Sussex R.
2. 1st Northamptons.
3. 2nd K.R.R.C.
4. 52nd Welch Regt.
5. T.M. Battery
6. No.2 Field Ambulance,
7. No. 3 Coy. Train,
8. 2nd Bde. Supply Offr,
9. Staff Captain,
10. Brigade Signal Officer,
11. P.R.O. No.2 Sub-Area,
12 & 13. 1st Division,
14. A.D.M.S.
15. A.P.M.
16 & 17. War Diary,
18. File.

BRIGADE ADMINISTRATIVE INSTRUCTIONS No.1.
In connection with the arrival of Young Soldiers' Battns.

4th March, 1919.

1. ACCOMMODATION.

(a) Incoming Battalions will be billetted as follows:

Battalion relieving 2nd Bn.R.Sussex Rt. - WITTERSCHLIEK, VOLMERSHOVEN and HEIDGEN.
" " 1st Northamptons. - DUISDORF and LESSENICH.
" " 2nd Bn.K.R.R.Corps. - ALFTER.

Each Battalion will prepare forthwith a billeting scheme for a Battalion 900 strong in the Area to be occupied by its relief.

(b) Outgoing units will be accommodated as follows:-

2nd Bn.R.Sussex Regt...................OEDEKOVEN and GIELSDORF.
1st Northamptonshire Regt..............)LENGSDORF.
No.2 Field Ambulance...................)
2nd Bn.K.R.R.Corps.....................DRANSDORF and MESSDORF.

Units will reconnoitre these Areas forthwith and draw up their billeting programmes.

2. SANITATION.

Construction of Latrines in new Areas will be put in hand forthwith by the Battalions who will occupy them. The R.Es. have been asked to supply material for the construction of 5 - 5 seater latrines per Battalion (or made latrines if available).
Units will be notified when and where these may be drawn.

3. RECEPTION OF NEW UNITS.

The Battalion to be relieved will move out of its present area either one or two days before the relieving Battalion is due to arrive, but will leave behind it all its Transport, complete with personnel. Further, the following personnel will be detailed as guides to bring the new Battalion from the detraining Station, put it into billets, and remain with it for a day or two till it becomes fully acquainted with its area:-

1 Officer and 1 N.C.O. for Hd.Qrs.
1 N.C.O. per Company.

This Officer and his N.C.Os. must be fully conversant with the details of the Billeting scheme made out in accordance with para.1 (a) above.
The Transport personnel will remain with the new unit until the latter has selected its own Transport personnel, when a complete handing over of all vehicles, animals and harness, etc., will take place, on completion of which personnel of relieved Battalion will rejoin its own unit.
In order that a hot meal may be ready for incoming Battalions, the relieved unit will on the day of arrival of its relieving unit send back to its old area sufficient personnel to get cookers, (which xxxxxxxxxxxxxxx will be left in Company areas selected in billeting scheme made out in accordance with para.1 (a) above-) going, and prepare hot Tea for the new Battalion. Tea, milk and sugar will be provided under Brigade arrangements.
As soon as incoming Battalions' Cooks have taken over, these personnel will rejoin its own Battalion.

4. MOBILE RESERVE OF AMMUNITION, etc.:

P.T.O.

2.

4. **MOBILE RESERVE OF AMMUNITION, etc.**

Outgoing Battalions will leave this in situ, under a guard, who will hand it over to incoming Battalions on arrival.

5. **CROCKERY.**

Crockery will be handed over to incoming Battalions.

6. **FIRE BUCKETS AND SENTRY BOXES.**

Will be handed over to incoming Battalions.

7. **DOCUMENTS.**

Information as to documents to be handed over will be communicated later.

8. No stores or equipment other than those detailed above will be left behind or handed over until further instructions are issued from this office.

[signature]

Captain, Staff Captain,
2nd Infantry Brigade.

Copies to:

2nd Bn. Royal Sussex Regiment.
1st Bn. Northamptonshire Regiment.
2nd Bn. King's Royal Rifle Corps.
2nd Trench Mortar Battery.
No.2 Field Ambulance.
Brigade Major.
2nd Brigade Supply Officer.
No.3 Coy. 1st Divisional Train.
52nd South Wales Borderers.
52nd Welch Regiment.
53rd Welch Regiment.
War Diary.

2nd Inf.Bde No.G16/17

2nd INFANTRY BRIGADE ORDER No. 263

Copy No. 20

1. Moves in accordance with table overleaf will take place on 31st March 1919.

2. The 2nd K.R.R.C. will send an advance party to take over billets from the 52nd South Wales Borderers at 09.00 hours 31st instant.

3. On completion of the moves the 51st Battalion Welch Regiment and 52nd South Wales Borderers will be transferred to the 2nd and 3rd Infantry Brigades respectively.

4. The 2nd K.R.R.C. and the 51st Welch Regiment will wire completion of moves to this Office.

30th March 1919.

Captain, Brigade Major,
2nd Infantry Brigade.

Issued through No.3 Signal Section at 14.00 hours.

DISTRIBUTION

Copy No.	1	G.O.C.
"	2	D.H.
"	3	S.C.
"	4	Bde. Signal Officer.
"	5	2nd Royal Sussex R.
"	6	1st Northamptonshire Regt.
"	7	2nd K.R.R.C.
"	8	51st Welch Regt.
"	9	52nd Welch Regt.
"	10	53rd Welch Regt.
"	11	2nd T.M.B.
"	12	No. 2 Field Ambulance
"	13	No. 3 Coy. Train.
"	14 & 15	Western Division.
"	16	A.D.M.S.
"	17	A.P.M.
"	18	2nd Inf.Bde.Supply Offr.
"	19	P.R.C. No.2 Sub Area
"	20 & 21	War Diary.
"	22	File
"	23	S.S Bdr

	From	To	Route	Remarks
2nd K.R.R.C.	DRANSDORF and HERSDORF	WITTERSCHLICK	Discretion of C.O.	Move not to be completed before 14.00 hours.
5 1st Welch Regt.	FLAMERSHEIM	MECKENHEIM	By road via HEUENBACH	
52nd South Wales Bde.	WITTERSCHLICK	ARLOFF and KIRSPENICH	Transport by road via FLERZHEIM PEPPENHOVEN OBR. DREES ESSIG cross-roads FLAMERSHEIM KIRSPENICH	Dismounted personnel by rail at an hour to be notified later.

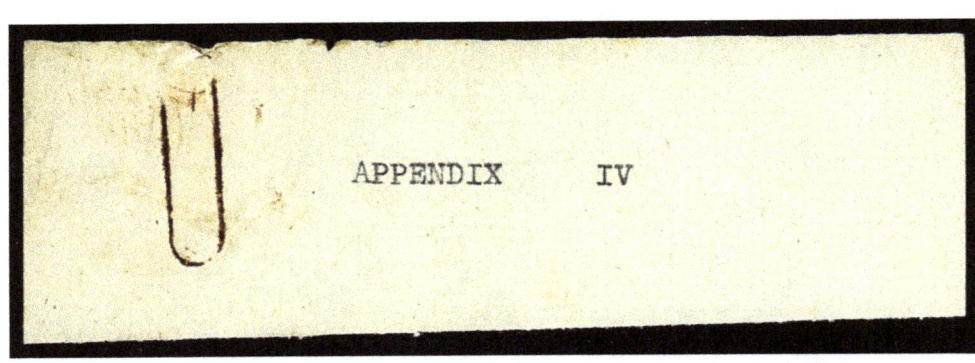

SECRET.

2ND INFANTRY BRIGADE No. G.10/10.

Copy No. 17

DEFENCE OF BONN

2nd INFANTRY BRIGADE INSTRUCTIONS No. 1.

1. In the event of action taking place on the perimeter of the COLOGNE Bridge-head, it may become necessary for the 32nd Division, at present providing the garrison of BONN, to move all its troops East of the RHINE.

    In such case, the 2nd Infantry Brigade, composed as under, will be required to take over the defence of BONN bridge and the duties, hereinafter provided for, in the neighbourhood of BONN.

    2nd Infantry Brigade.

        2nd Royal Sussex Regiment.
        52nd Welch Regiment.
        2nd K.R.R.C.
        2nd Light T.M. Battery.
        1 Section No. 76 Field Company R.E.
        No.2 Field Ambulance.

    (NOTE:- The places of the 2nd Royal Sussex Regiment and the 2nd K.R.R.C. in this Scheme will be taken by their relieving units from home on arrival.)

2. The task of the 2nd Infantry Brigade would then be:-

    (a) To ensure communication across the Bridge at BONN, and to close the Bridge to any unauthorised persons.

    (b) To maintain order in the Town of BONN.

3. A plan of the Town of BONN, scale 1/10,000; 96th Infantry Brigade Scheme "Defence of BONN Bridge"; and 96th Infantry Brigade "Arrangements in the case of Riots in BONN", are attached hereto as Appendices I, II and III respectively. Except in so far as they may be at variance with anything in these instructions contained, the provisions of Appendices II and III will be adhered to in carrying out the above task.

4. Should there be no actual disturbance in BONN, units, on receipt of message "Perimeter", will take action as follows:-

    (a) The 52nd Welch Regiment will proceed forthwith and relieve the 12th Loyal North Lancashire Regiment (Pioneers) on the BONN Bridge (see Appendix II, paras.5, 6 and 7).

    (NOTE:- In the event of the 12th L.N.Lancs not having already taken over the BONN Bridge defences, the 52nd Welch Regiment will proceed to the MUSEUM KONIG, CODLENZ STRASSE (Appendix I, C,5) and take over billets from 15th Lancs. Fusiliers, at once despatching a party of 1

/Officer

- 1 -

Officer, 2 Sergeants, 2 Corporals, and 18 Privates, to relieve the Guard at the Western end of the BONN Bridge.)

(b) The 2nd K.R.R.C. will proceed to the ARTILLERIE KASERNE, in the RHEINDORFER STRASSE (Appendix I, I.8), taking over billets from the 2nd Battalion Manchester Regiment, and finding the following Guards and Duties forthwith:-

Serial No.	Composition	Location and Duties	Where Billeted
1.	Two Companies	Picquet under A.P.M. BONN.	FORT BILDUNGS SCHULE G. 5, 6.
2.	3 N.C.O's 10 Privates	ADOLF PLATZ, BONN, H.6 Lorry Park Guard.	KONIG WILHELM KASERNE, RHEINDORFER STRASSE, BONN, H.8.
3.	1 N.C.O. 6 Privates	NUSS ALLEE, BONN, F.3 Lorry Park Guard	Hut near Lorry Park off NUSS ALLEE.
4.	3 N.C.O's 18 other ranks	Guards over Goods Station, BONN. H.5.	In Station.

The above Duties will be taken over from whatever Battalion of the 96th Infantry Brigade is finding the Town Guard for the week.

(c) The 2nd Royal Sussex Regiment will proceed to the INFANTERIE KASERNE, ENDENICH STRASSE, (Appendix I, D.4), and take over billets from the 16th Lancs. Fusiliers. The Battalion will stand fast in billets ready on receipt of orders to mount the Guards provided for in Appendix III, para. 7, sub-paras. a, b, c, and d.

(d) The 2nd Infantry Brigade H.Q. will close at MEDINGHOVEN BURG and re-open on arrival at OFFICIER SPEISEAMT, RHEINDORFER STRASSE, Appendix I H.8

(e) The O.C. 2nd Light T.M. Battery will despatch 1 Section of guns to report to O.C. 52nd Welch Regt. on the BONN Bridge, and will report with his remaining two guns at 2nd Infantry Brigade H.Q., RHEINDORFER STRASSE.

(f) The Section of No. 76 Field Company R.E. from WITTERSCHLICK will proceed independently to the Bridge and take over from the Section of R.E. under the abutment at the Eastern end of the Bridge (see Appendix II, para 7) reporting to the O.C. 52nd Welch Regiment afterwards.

(g) No.2 Field Ambulance will take over billets and Duties from 91st Field Ambulance, at NORD SCHULE, RHEINDORFER STRASSE (Appendix I. H. 7, 8).

5.   Completion of the above moves will be reported immediately to 2nd Infantry Brigade H.Q.

6.   In the event, however, of disturbances in BONN coinciding with action on the perimeter, units will receive the message "Perimeter Riots", and will take action as follows:-

   (a)   The 52nd Welch Regiment will act as laid down in para. 4 sub-para (a).

   (b)   The 2nd K.R.R.C. will march to BONN, despatching on the way one Company to relieve a company of 2nd Manchester Regiment in the Electricity & Gas Works, near the BONN Goods Station (Appendix I, H.4). On arrival in BONN, serials 1, 2 and 3, (but not 4) of the list of Guards in para 4, sub-para (b) will be despatched to their several duties; and Battalion H.Q., together with the remainder of the Battalion will proceed to the MARKT (Appendix I, F. 6.), and report to Brigade H.Q. at the RATHAUS. As soon as the relief of the Company of the 2nd Manchester Regt. in the Electricity & Gas Works is completed, a message will be sent by the 2nd K.R.R.C. Company Commander to the Guard on the Goods Station (Serial No.4, para 4, sub-para. (b) hereof) authorising it to return to its Battalion.

   (c)   The 2nd Royal Sussex Regiment will forthwith take over the Guards provided for in Appendix III, para. 7, sub-paras. a, b, c and d, establishing Battn. H.Q. at the Railway Station.

   (d)   The 2nd Infantry Brigade H.Q. will close at MEDINGHOVEN BURG and re-open on arrival at the RATHAUS, in the MARKT (Appendix I, F.6).

   (e)   O.C. 2nd Light T.M. Battery will despatch 1 Section of 2 guns to report to the 52nd Welch Regiment, BONN Bridge, and will report with his remaining 2 guns at the 2nd Infantry Brigade H.Q., RATHAUS.

   (f)   The Section of No. 76 Field Company R.E. will act as as laid down in para. 4, sub-para. (f).

   (g)   No.2 Field Ambulance will act as laid down in para. 4 sub-para (g).

7.   Completion of the above moves will be immediately reported to 2nd Infantry Brigade H.Q.

8.   Unit Commanders will arrange for the necessary reconnaissances to be carried out forthwith.

9.   Signal and administrative instructions, and instructions dealing with Artillery and Machine Gun co-operation, if available, will be issued separately.

0.   ACKNOWLEDGE.

                                        Captain, Brigade Major,
                                          2nd Infantry Brigade.

Issued through No.3 Signal Section at
17.00 hours 12th March 1919.

Distribution

	Copy No. 1	........G. O. C.
	" " 2	........B. M.
	" " 3	........S. C.
	" " 4	........Bde. Signals Officer
✷	" " 5	........2nd Royal Sussex Regt.
✷	" " 6	........52nd Welch Regt.
✷	" " 7	........2nd K. R. R. C.
✷	" " 8	........T. M. Battery, (2nd Light)
	" " 9	........Section of 76 Field Coy R.E. at WITTERSCHLICK.
✷	" " 10	........No. 2 Field Ambulance.
	" " 11 & 12	....1st Division.
	" " 13	........A. D. M. S.
	" " 14	........A. P. M.
✢	" " 15	........96th Infantry Brigade.
	" " 16	........2nd Inf. Bde. Supply Officer.
	" " 17 & 18	...War Diary.
	" " 19	........File.

✷ Appendix I, only issued to starred distributants.

✢ No Appendices issued.

SECRET

APPENDIX II

TO

2nd INFANTRY BRIGADE INSTRUCTIONS No. 1.

96th Inf.Bde. No.G.1021/2/7.

DEFENCE OF BONN BRIDGE.

RESERVE INFANTRY BRIGADE - 2ND DIVISION.

1. In the event of operations East of the Rhine it will be necessary to safeguard BONN Bridge from wilful damage so as to ensure free transit across the Rhine and also to close the Bridge to any unauthorised persons.

2. The conditions assumed in the event of hostile action against BONN Bridge are:-

   (a) That the enemy has rifles, machine guns, bombs and explosives, but not artillery.

   (b) That the garrison must be prepared to hold out for about 48 hours.

3. The Bridge at BONN consists of three spans with a sloping roadway at each end. At the eastern end this roadway is carried on seven brick arches and at the Western end on one arch.

   On the Bridge itself are four pairs of towers which are built over the piers that support the main girders. The towers on the shore piers have entrances from the ~~Bridge itself~~ Embankment and gateways, not bullet proof on the Bridge itself.

   Houses exist on either bank in close proximity to the Bridge entrances.

4. The most vulnerable points of the Bridge are the shore ends of the main girders which can be reached from the embankments on both sides of the river.

   In addition to holding the Bridge itself it will be necessary to hold the houses at each end.

5. The garrison detailed for the defence of the Bridge is:-

   19th L.N.Lancs. Regt. (Pioneers) with all Lewis Guns of the Battalion and a minimum strength of 400 all ranks.
   1 Section R.E. from Field Coy. at PUTZCHEN.
   1 Section 18-pdrs. from Reserve Brigade, R.F.A.

6. Troops as above will on receipt of orders from Divisional Headquarters move at once to XXX Bridge where the O.C., 19th L.N.Lancs.Regt. will take over the defence of the Bridge, and come under orders of G.O.C., Reserve Infantry Brigade whose Headquarters will be established at the RATHAUS.

7. DISTRIBUTION OF TROOPS.

   ARTILLERY. 1 Section of 18-pdrs will take up a position on the right bank of the Rhine about 100 yards North of the Eastern end of the Bridge and report to

O.C., 19th L.N.Lancs. Regt.

R.E. The Section of R.E. will halt under the abutment at the Eastern End of the Bridge, report to O.C., 19th L.N.Lancs. Regt. and act under his orders.

Their role in the defence will depend on whether the trouble is on the left or right bank of the Rhine.

INFANTRY For the purposes of defence the Bridge is divided into two sectors at the centre.

Eastern Sector The Eastern half of the Bridge and the houses and buildings bounded by the line from PONTOON Bridge - WILHELM STRASSE - KAISER STRASSE - OCHPANN STRASSE - River Bank North of Bridge.

Western Sector. The Western half of the Bridge and the houses and buildings bounded by a line from PONTOON BRIDGE North of Guard Room - JOSEPH STRASSE - DOETSCH STRASSE - MUHLEN GASSE - To River Bank South of Bridge.

Eastern Sector:- Garrison to consist of two Companies of 19th L.N.Lancs. Regt. disposed as follows:-

No.1 Company
 1 Platoon in East Tower on Bridge.
 1 Platoon in Abutment Tower.
 1 Platoon in houses at North end of RHEIN STRASSE.
 1 Platoon at corner of RHEIN and WILHELM STRASSE.
 Company Headquarters in East Abutment Tower.

No.2 Company
 1 Platoon at corner of KAISER and WILHELM STRASSE.
 1 Platoon at junction of KAISER and BRUCKEN STRASSE.
 1 Platoon at corner of OCHPANN and KAISER STRASSE.
 1 Platoon in support in BRUCKEN STRASSE.
 Company Headquarters with support Platoon.

Western Sector:- Garrison to consist of two Companies of 19th L.N.Lancs. Regt. disposed as follows:-

No.3 Company
 1 Platoon in West Tower on Bridge.
 1 Platoon in Abutment Tower.
 1 Platoon (less 1 Section) at corner of RHEINWERFT and JOSEPH STRASSE.
 1 Section at East end of narrow lane 40 yards North of Abutment.
 1 Platoon (less 1 Section) at corner of RHEINWERFT and MUHLEN GASSE.
 1 Section in Tower 70 yards South of ABUTMENT.
 Company Headquarters near junction of BRUCKEN STRASSE and DOETSCH STRASSE.

No.4 Company
 1 Platoon at corner of JOSEPH and DOETSCH STRASSE.
 1 Platoon at corner of DOETSCH STRASSE and MUHLEN GASSE.
 1 Platoon at junction of BRUCKEN - DOETSCH STRASSE.

/No.4 Company (Contd)

No. 4 Company.   1 Platoon in Support at Guard Room.
    (Contd)   Company Headquarters with Support
                        Platoon.

LEWIS GUNS.   Positions for certain Lewis Guns for
special purposes, and their lines of fire, are shewn in
red on the attached map.

DRESSING STATIONS.   A Dressing Station will be established
at whichever end of the Bridge the trouble is taking place.
    In the event of trouble at both ends at the same time,
an extra M.O., will be sent to establish a second Aid Post.

8.   In the event of trouble in BONN coinciding with action
on the perimeter, all troops of the 32nd Division may be
required for operations East of the River (as outlined in
Provisional Defence Scheme).   In this case the defence of
BONN Bridge will be taken over as early as possible from the
12th L.F.Lancs. Regt. by troops of the 2nd Infantry Brigade,
1st Division.
    On relief the 12th L.F.Lancs. Regt. will concentrate in
the Eastern end of BEUEL and the Artillery and Engineers will
rejoin their units.

9.   The following ammunition etc., has been stored in equal
proportions at the Guard House at the BONN end of the Bridge and
at the Headquarters of the 5/6th Royal Scots at the BEUEL end of
the Bridge:-

    120,000 rounds S.A.A. - 300 rounds per man.
    36,000 rounds S.A.A. for Lewis Guns.
    180 boxes Mills grenades.
    2,000 Sandbags.
    150 knife rests.
    30 bundles barbed wire.
    12 crowbars.
    12 buckets each with 100 feet rope.
    Rations for 400 men for two days.

    These will eventually be distributed as follows:-

    One third S.A.A., 60 boxes Mills, 6 crowbars and half
the rations, sandbags and wire, will remain in the Guard House
at the BONN end of the Bridge and similar quantities at the
present Headquarters of the 5/6th Royal Scots; the remainder with
the buckets and rope will be stored in the Towers nearest the
banks.
    Orders as to the storage of knife rests will be issued
later.
    Positions of knife rests are shown in attached map in
blue.
    The garrisons of the sectors are responsible for putting
out the knife rests on the first alarm.

10.   Large scale maps of the Bridge will be issued to those
immediately concerned, showing the general organisation and the
places where defences would be required.

11.   The scheme for the defence of BONN Bridge will come
into force in the event of riots in BONN whether connected or
not with hostile operations elsewhere.

                                                /12.

12.   O.C., 12th L.N.Lancs. Regt. will be O.C., Bridge, with Headquarters in the Western Tower.

13.   <u>Communication</u> Details of communication will be issued later as an Appendix.

14.   If available, a section of Trench Mortars will be sent to reinforce the garrisons.

15.   Houses in defended area will be cleared of inhabitants as quickly as possible.
        They may be turned out of the area or collected in suitable places, under cover, in the defended area at each end of the bridge.   No civilian is to cross the bridge under any circumstances once the order to defend it has reached the Guard.

16.   O.C., Garrison, at each end of the bridge, will arrange for frequent patrolling for some distance outside the defended area of all roads leading into it.

SECRET.

APPENDIX III
TO
2nd INFANTRY BRIGADE INSTRUCTIONS No. 1.

6TH Inf. Bde. No.1021/8/4.

ARRANGEMENTS IN THE CASE OF RIOTS IN
---BONN---
RESERVE BRIGADE - 32ND DIVISION

1. All troops quartered in BONN will be under command of and receive orders from G.O.C., Reserve Infantry Brigade, 32nd Division.

2. Individuals will at once return to the billets of their Unit.

3. On receipt of warning Units (except as stated in para. 7 and the usual weekly guards, in the case of the Battalion who is finding them) will parade in "Battle Order" i.e., steel helmets, box respirators, haversacks with iron rations, filled water-bottles, 120 rounds per man, and Lewis Guns with drums complete. Stretchers will be taken.

4. The following are Alarm Posts of Units:-

   15th Lancs. Fusrs. (less Guards detailed in para 7.)
   MUSEUM, GOBLENZER STRASSE.

   16th Lancs. Fusrs. (Less Guards detailed in para 7.)
   INFANTRY BARRACKS, ENDENICH STRASSE.

   2nd Manchester Regt (less Guards detailed in para. 7)
   ARTILLERIE KASERNE, RHEIN DORFER STRASSE.

5. (a) Officers, their servants and clerks of II Corps H.Q., will assemble at the KOENIGS OF HOTEL.
   (b) Officers, clerks, servants, etc, of 32nd Divisional Headquarters will assemble at Divisional Headquarters in POPPELSDORFER ALLEE.

6. The scheme for the defence of BONN Bridge, laid down in Appendix II to 32nd Division Defence Scheme, will come into force.
   The 12th L.N.Lancs. Regt. (Pioneers), 1 Section Field Company, R.E., and 1 Section 18-pdr. Battery, R.F.A., will on receipt of orders from Divnl. Headquarters, move at once to BONN Bridge where they will take over the defence of the bridge and come under the orders of G.O.C., Reserve Infantry Brigade commanding the troops in BONN.

7. Immediately warning order is received the following Guards will be mounted without waiting for orders from Brigade:-

   15th Lancs Fusrs. (or 16th Lancs. Fusrs. if 15th Lancs are finding Town Guards for the week):-

   (a) 2 Platoons between the GOBLENZER TOR and passage leading from HOFGARTEN to RHEIN STRAND.

- 1 -

/ (b)

(b) 1 Company (less 2 Platoons) at RATHAUS in the MARKET SQUARE.
(c) 1 Company in the MUNSTERPLATZ and to occupy the Post and Telegraph Office.
(d) 1 Battalion (less 2 Companies) in and around the Railway Station.

2nd Manchester Regt. 1 Company at the Gas and Electricity Works at GUTERBAHOF.

8. Units not detailed for the above will picket road junctions in the immediate vicinity of their alarm posts and will prevent all civilian crowds passing.

Picquets at road junctions will consist of a complete Platoon with Lewis Guns.

9. The Headquarters of the G.O.C., Troops (G.O.C., Reserve Infantry Brigade, 32nd Division) will be established at the RATHAUS in liaison with the Commandant, BONN, and will consist of the following:-

> G. O. C.
> Brigade Major,
> Signalling Officer,
> 1 Clerk
> 6 Runners
> 2 Signal Operators
> 3 Officers' Servants.
> Grooms and Horses.

The rest of Brigade Headquarters will remain in their present quarters.

10. In the event of trouble in BONN coinciding with action on the perimeter, all troops of the 32nd Division may be required for operations east of the River (as outlined in Provisional Defence Scheme). In this case the 1st Division will take over the defence of BONN Bridge and the duties in BONN from the 15th L.F.Lancs. Regt., and Reserve Brigade, 32nd Division. The G.O.C., 2nd Infantry Brigade, 1st Division, on completion of relief, will take over command of the troops in BONN from G.O.C., Reserve Brigade, 32nd Division.

The 1st Division have detailed the following troops to proceed to BONN on receipt of orders:-

> 2nd Infantry Brigade
> 1 Section, Field Coy, R.E.
> No. 2 Field Ambulance.

On approach of the 2nd Infantry Brigade, Battalions will be ordered to send guides to rendezvous which will be notified at the time.

11. Action as above will be taken by Os. C., Units immediately on receipt of the word "Riots". This will be issued from Brigade by telephone and confirmed in writing.

12. All units will send two Runners, with bicycles, to report

/to

to the Brigade Major at the RATHAUS in the MARKET SQUARE.

13.   O.C., 91st Field Ambulance will make the necessary arrangements for establishing a First Aid Post at or near the RATHAUS.

ADDENDUM No 1 TO 2nd INFANTRY BRIGADE ADMINISTRATIVE
INSTRUCTIONS No 1.
------------------------ -----------------

5th March 1919.

TRANSPORT.
In order to carry on the work of outgoing Battalions, including the drawing of supplies from Refilling Point, the following transport will be placed at the disposal of Os.C. outgoing, by Os.C. incoming, Battalions :-

4 Limbered G.S.Wagons.

This transport will be merely loaned temporarily to outgoing units, and will be manned in the first place by personnel of the outgoing unit, and later, when the complete handing over referred to in para 3 of 2nd Brigade Administrative Instructions No 1 has been carried out, by transport personnel of incoming units. It will stay with the remainder of the transport in the old area but be at the call of the outgoing Battalion.

Should outgoing Battalions from time to time need more transport than legislated for herein, application will be made to Brigade Headquarters stating purpose for which required.

(signed)

Captain, Staff Captain,
2nd Infantry Brigade.

Copies to :-

    2nd Bn. Royal Sussex Regt.
    1st Bn. Northamptonshire Regt.
    2nd Bn. K.R.R.Corps.
    2nd Trench Mortar Battery.
    No 2 Field Ambulance.
    Brigade Major.
    2nd Brigade Supply Officer.
    No 3 Coy. 1st Divl. Train.
    52nd South Wales Borderers.
    52nd Welch Regiment.
    53rd Welch Regiment.
    War Diary.

S E C R E T.   2nd Inf. Bde. No. C.10/12

Copy No......20........

DEFENCE OF BONN

2nd Infantry Brigade INSTRUCTIONS No. 2.

ARTILLERY AND MACHINE GUN CO-OPERATION

1. In addition to the troops detailed in para. 1 of 2nd Infantry Brigade Instructions No. 1,

    1 Section 113 Battery, 25th Bde. R.F.A. (18 pdr), and "D" Company 1st Battn. Machine Gun Corps,

    have been placed at the disposal of the Brigadier General Commanding the 2nd Infantry Brigade.

2. On the receipt of the message "Perimeter" these units will act as follows:-

    (a) The Section of 18 pdrs. will proceed to the BONN Bridge and take over accommodation and positions from 1 Section 32nd D.A. (see para 7 Appendix II of 2nd Infantry Brigade Instructions No. 1) the Section Commander reporting at once to the O.C. 52nd Welch Regiment on the Bridge. In the event of the defences of the Bridge not having yet been manned (see note to para. 4(a) of 2nd Infantry Brigade Instructions No.1) he will report the location of his guns to the O.C. 52nd Welch Regiment at the MUSEUM KONIG, COBLENZ STRASSE.

    (b) "D" Company 1st Battn. Machine Gun Corps, will march to BONN and take up billets at the KAISER WILHELM KASERNE, RHEINDORFER STRASSE, despatching en route 2 Sections to report forthwith to the O.C. 52nd Welch Regiment on the BONN Bridge. In the event of the Bridge not having yet been manned, a Liaison Officer, with a cyclist orderly, will be sent to the O.C. 52nd Welch Regiment at the MUSEUM KONIG, COBLENZ STRASSE, and the 2 Sections will rejoin their Company at the KAISER WILHELM KASERNE.

    On arrival in billets, the Company will stand by ready on receipt of orders to act as laid down in para 3 (b) hereof.

3. On receipt of the message "Perimeter Riots", the action of the above units will be as under:-

    (a) The Section of 18 pdrs. will trot to BONN Bridge Bridge, and act as in para. 2(a) hereof.

/(b)

(b) "D" Company 1st Battn. Machine Gun Corps, will march to BONN, despatching 2 Sections to the BONN Bridge, as in para. 2 (b), and 1 Section to take up positions, under O.C. 2nd Royal Sussex Regiment, covering the COBLENZ STRASSE, and the POPPELSDORFER ALLEE. "D" Company, 1st Battn. Machine Gun Corps (less 3 Sections) will report to 2nd Infantry Brigade Headquarters, at the RATHAUS in the MARKT.

4. Units will proceed complete with first line transport, carrying ammunition in the case of the Artillery on the scale of 100 rounds per gun. A dump of Artillery ammunition will if possible be arranged in the neighbourhood of the Bridge. Sections of Machine Guns will be accompanied by their fighting limbers, the remaining transport of the Company being parked in the neighbourhood of Company H.Q.

5. Unit Commanders will arrange to carry out the necessary reconnaissances forthwith.

6. ACKNOWLEDGE.

[signature]

Captain, Brigade Major,
2nd Infantry Brigade.

20th March, 1919.

Issued through No.3 Signal Section at 13.00 hours.

DISTRIBUTION

```
Copy No. 1........G.O.C.
  "    "  2........B.M.
  "    "  3........S.C.
  "    "  4........Bde. Signal Officer.
  "    "  5........2nd Royal Sussex Regt.
  "    "  6........52nd Welch Regiment.
  "    "  7........2nd M.R.A.C.
  "    "  8........2nd Light T.M. Battery.
  "    "  9........Section of 76 Field Coy. R.E. at WI-TERSCHLICK.
  "    "  10.......No.2 Field Ambulance.
  "    "  11.&.12..Western Division.
  "    "  13.......A.D.M.S.
  "    "  14.......A.P.M.
  "    "  15.......96th Infantry Brigade.
  "    "  16.......2nd Inf. Bde. Supply Officer.
  "    "  17.......Lt.W.Chambers, 113 Bty, 25th Bde. R.F.A.
  "    "  18......."D" Coy. 1st Battn. M.G. Corps.
  "    "  19 & 20..War Diary.
  "    "  21.......File.
```

SECRET.   2nd Inf.Bde.No.A.10/...
                                              Copy No. 20

DEFENCE OF BONN.

2nd Infantry Brigade   Instructions No 3.

ADMINISTRATIVE. (Provisional.)

1. **DRESS.**
   On receipt of the warning message, whether it be "Perimeter" or "Perimeter Riots", Battalions will immediately complete men to 120 rounds per man from ammunition held in Quartermaster Stores for that purpose. Troops will parade in fighting order.

2. **TRANSPORT.**
   (a). O.C. No.3.Coy Western Division Train will, on receipt of warning message, send Units baggage wagons to report at Units present Headquarters.

   (b). In the case of action on the perimeter with no disturbances in BONN, all transport will accompany Battalions and take over transport lines of "opposite number" Battalions of 96th Brigade.

   (c). In the case of disturbances in X.., 1st line transport only will accompany Battalion and will, at the discretion of Battalion Commanders either proceed to transport lines of opposite number Battalions of 96th Brigade, or remain with Battalion Headquarters. Remaining transport including baggage wagons, will stay at present Battalions Headquarters ready to proceed to BONN on receipt of orders from Battalion Commanders.

   (d). All Field Ambulance Transport will, in either case move with unit.

3. **STORES etc.**
   All packs, blankets and stores not taken with Battalions will be collected into central dumps, one for Battalion Headquarters and one for each Company, one N.C.O., and three men provided with two days rations being left in charge of each dump. One Officer and two N.C.Os in addition will be left behind by each Battalion to supervise it's dumps.
   Trench Mortar Battery will form one central dump leaving one N.C.O. and one man in charge.

4. **BRIGADE RESERVE OF AMMUNITION.**
   The R.A.O.C. have been asked to hold the following in readiness to proceed on receipt of warning message to DUISDORF where a guard of 1 N.C.O. and six men to be detailed by O.C. 52nd Welsh Regt will meet convoy, and conduct it to 2nd Brigade Headquarters X..

Lewis Gun magazines filled.	... ...	4 per gun = 384.
Bundle packed S.A.A.	... ...	50 Boxes.
Ordinary, S.A.A.	... ...	50 Boxes.
Grenades. No.36.	... ...	128 Boxes.
T.N.C.	... ...	200 rounds.
Grenades No.27 (Smoke) ...	... ...	40 Boxes (with bursters and rods.)

/5. SUPPLIES.

5. **SUPPLIES.** Refilling point, from the day after the Brigade's move to BONN will be at the Gas Works near BONN goods Station.

6. **ACKNOWLEDGE.**

G.B.Bruce
Captain Staff Captain.
2nd Infantry Brigade.

27.3.1919.

Issued through No.2 Signal Section at 16-00 hours.

DISTRIBUTION.

Copy No. 1..............G.O.C.
"   "   2..............B..
"   "   3..............S.C.
"   "   4..............Bde. Signal Officer.
"   "   5..............2nd Royal Sussex Regt.
"   "   6..............5?nd Welsh Regiment.
"   "   7..............2nd King's Royal Rifle Corps.
"   "   8..............2nd L.T.M. Battery.
"   "   9..............Section of 76 Field Coy R.E. at WOTTERSCHLICK.
"   "   10.............No 2 Field Ambulance.
"   "   11.&.12.........Western Division.
"   "   13.............A.D.M.S.
"   "   14.............A.P.M.
"   "   15.............96th Infantry Brigade.
"   "   16.............2nd Inf. Bde. Supply Officer.
"   "   17.............Lt.W.CHAMBERS, 113 Bty, 25th Bde R.F.A.
"   "   18............."D" Coy. 1st Battn. M.G.Corps.
"   "   19.&.20.........War Diary.
"   "   21.............File.

SECRET

2nd Inf. Bde. No. G.10/15.

52nd Welsh Regiment.

Reference Map of BONN 1/10,000, Appendix 1 of
2nd Infantry Brigade Instructions No.1.

The Brigade Commander, having made a personal reconnaissance of the Bonn Bridge Defences, considers that the existing Scheme makes insufficient allowance for elasticity and depth in defence, and further, that certain buildings of tactical importance require to be included.

In his opinion the perimeter of the defence should be, on the West Bank, NEUSTRASSE, ENGEL STRASSE, JOSEPH STRASSE, HUNDS GASSE, RHEIN GASSE (including the Hotel RHEINECK), with patrols pushed out towards the MARKT, and, on the East Bank, KAISER CONRAD STRASSE, BRUCKEN STRASSE, LIMPERICHER STRASSE, TALWED STEINER STRASSE, to the River Bank. In addition to providing the necessary depth, this rearrangement contains the network of streets and alleys (some of which do not appear on the map) in the neighbourhood of the KATH.KIRCHE and St. JOSEPHS KRANKENHAUS in D.8.

The Brigadier does not wish to lay down anything hard and fast as to the disposition of troops in these areas except that there should be no troops other than the attached Machine Gun Sections on the Bridge itself, (2 Infantry Companies being told off for the defences on either side of the river). He suggests, however, that the Hotel RHEINECK should be held with a Platoon, the BRUCKEN STRASSE inclusive to the Southern Company. The Companies on this bank might disposed with 3 Platoons on or about the perimeter, to provide patrols and guard cross-roads. and BRUCKENSTRASSE. On the East Bank the Inter-Company boundary might be the WILHEIM STRASSE inclusive to the Northern Company, who would then be responsible for covering the open spaces and road junctions in the neighbourhood of the projected MARKT PLATZ (D.8), thus freeing the Southern Company to watch the road confluence from the South East. As before, he thinks 3 Platoons per Company on or about the perimeter, and 1 Platoon in reserve, would meet the tactical requirements; attention would, however, need to be paid by the Northern Company to the RHINE foreshore West of the Bahnhof de BROITAL (D.8) and to the Light Railway.

Will you therefore please arrage to carry out the necessary reconnaissances with your Company Commanders forthwith, and forward your views on the above proposals to reach this office by 18-00 hours 2nd April, attaching to your report a plan showing the proposed disposition of your troops, Machine Guns and Lewis Guns, in detail, and the location of proposed Battalion Headquarters and Company Headquarters.

With regard to the transport which will accompany you to the Bridge (see Instructions No.3.) please reconnoitre and report on suitable transport lines and accommodation within the perimeter of the defences as laid down above.

                                                Captain, Brigade Major.
                                                  2nd Infantry Brigade.

27th March, 1919.

Copy to:- Western Division.

Army Form W.3091.

Cover for Documents.

SECRET

Nature of Enclosures.

WAR DIARY of

2nd WESTERN INFANTRY BRIGADE

(formerly - 2nd INFANTRY BRIGADE)

From 1st April, 1919 to 30th April, 1919.

Brigadier General,
Commanding 2nd Western Infantry Brigade.

Notes, or Letters written.

SECRET

Army Form C. 2118.

Original

WAR DIARY
INTELLIGENCE SUMMARY.
(Erase heading not required.)

Place	Date	Hour	Summary of Events and Information	Remarks and references to Appendices
	APRIL			
	10th		The Cadre of the 2nd Battalion The King's Royal Rifle Corps proceeded to England.	
	12th		The Cadre of the 2nd Battalion The Royal Sussex Regiment proceeded to England.	
			In accordance with Army Routine Order No. 2600 dated 12th April 1919, the 2nd Infantry Brigade was re-named the 2nd Western Infantry Brigade.	
	15th		Lieut: (T/Captain) R.C.Berkeley, M.C. (Rifle Brigade), Brigade Major, 2nd Infantry Brigade, proceeded to England for demobilization, his successor being Captain G. Wingfield Stratford, M.C. (Royal West Kent Regiment).	
	30th		The Commander in Chief, British Army of the Rhine, inspected the 2nd Western Infantry Brigade (less the 5 1st Battalion The Welsh Regiment) at DUISDORF.	
			Training during the month consisted of re-organisation of Battalions, drill, section training, preliminary musketry and education.	

Brigadier General,
Commanding 2nd Western Infantry Brigade.

ORIGINAL

(6339) Wt. W160/M3016 1,500,000 10/17 McA & W Ltd (E1898) Forms W3091.   Army Form W.3091.

Cover for Documents.

S E C R E T

Nature of Enclosures.

W A R   D I A R Y

of

2nd WESTERN INFANTRY BRIGADE.

from 1st May 1919,.....to 31st May, 1919.

--------oOo---------

[signature]

Brigadier General,
Commanding 2nd Western Infantry Brigade.

Notes, or Letters written.

ORIGINAL.

Army Form C. 2118.

WAR DIARY
or
INTELLIGENCE-SUMMARY.   SECRET

(Erase heading not required.)

Instructions regarding War Diaries and Intelligence Summaries are contained in F. S. Regs., Part II. and the Staff Manual respectively. Title pages will be prepared in manuscript.

Place	Date	Hour	Summary of Events and Information	Remarks and references to Appendices
MEDINGHOVEN	MAY			
	1st		2 Companies of the 51st Battalion The Welsh Regiment, and 2 Companies of the 52nd Battalion the Welsh Regiment commenced firing the General Musketry Course.	Good
	16th		The second 2 Companies of the 51st Battalion, and the second 2 Companies of the 52nd Battalion, The Welsh Regiment commenced firing the General Musketry Course.	Good
			Companies not at Musketry carried out Section Training.	

3rd June, 1919.

P.B.Master.

Brigadier General,
Commanding 2nd Western Infantry Brigade.

S E C R E T

W A R   D I A R Y

of

2nd Western Infantry Brigade Headquarters.

From 1st June, 1919 to 30th June, 1919.

Lieut: Colonel,
Commanding 2nd Western Infantry Brigade

WAR DIARY
or
INTELLIGENCE SUMMARY.

(Erase heading not required.)

2nd Western Infantry Brigade   Army Form C. 2118.

Place	Date	Hour	Summary of Events and Information	Remarks and references to Appendices
MEDINGHOVEN	JUNE 1st		Location	
			2nd Western Infantry Brigade Headquarters....... MEDINGHOVEN.	
			51st Battalion Welsh Regiment................... MECKENHEIM.	
			52nd Battalion Welsh Regiment................... DUISDORF.	
			53rd Battalion Welsh Regiment................... ALFTER.	
			2nd Western Trench Mortar Battery............... MESSDORF.	
			No. 2 Field Ambulance........................... LENGSDORF.	
			No. 3 Company, Western Divisional Train......... LIPEKOVEN.	
	9th		Colonel (T/Brigadier General) T.O.Marden, C.B., C.M.G., granted 6 days' Special Leave to England. Lieut: Colonel C.S.Owen, C.M.G., D.S.O., 51st Battalion Welsh Regiment assuming temporary command of the Brigade.	Apx
	13th		Colonel (T/Brigadier General) T.O.Marden, C.B., C.M.G., promoted to the rank of Major General.	Apx
	15th		Major General T.O.Marden, C.B., C.M.G., resumed command of the Brigade.	Apx
	17th		Orders were received for the Brigade to move in accordance with a Scheme of concentration of the British Army of the Rhine, preparatory to advancing in the event of the peace negotiations failing.	Apx
	18th		51st Battalion Welsh Regiment marched from MECKENHEIM to BONN. Guards from all Battalions took over duties from the Eastern and Lancashire Divisions.	Apx
	19th		2nd Western Infantry Brigade Headquarters marched from MEDINGHOVEN to BONN.	Apx
			51st Battalion Welsh Regiment marched from BONN to TROISDORF.	
			52nd Battalion Welsh Regiment marched from DUISDORF to BONN.	
			53rd Battalion Welsh Regiment marched from ALFTER to BONN.	
			2nd Western Trench Mortar Battery marched from MESSDORF to BONN.	
			No. 2 Field Ambulance marched from LENGSDORF to BONN.	
			No.3 Western Divisional Train marched from LIPEKOVEN to BONN.	

WAR DIARY 2nd Western Infantry Brigade

or

INTELLIGENCE SUMMARY.

(Erase heading not required.)

Army Form C. 2118.

Place	Date	Hour	Summary of Events and Information	Remarks and references to Appendices
MEDINGHOVEN	JUNE 19th		No.3 Section 76 Field Company R.E., and "B" Company, 1st Battalion Machine Gun Corps joined the Brigade Group in BONN.	Apx
BONN	20th		504 Battery, Royal Field Artillery, joined the Brigade Group in BONN.	Apx
	23rd		Major General T.O.Marden, C.B., C.M.G., assumed temporary Command of Western Division. Lieut: Colonel J.R.M.Minshull Ford, D.S.O., l.C., 52nd Battalion Welsh Regiment assumed temporary command of the Brigade.	Apx
	28th		Peace having been signed, orders were received for the Brigade to return to its former area.	Apx
	29th		51st Battalion Welsh Regiment marched from TROISDORF to BONN. All guards found by units of the Brigade in Eastern and Lancashire Division area were relieved and rejoined their Battalions.	Apx
MEDINGHOVEN	30th		2nd Western Infantry Brigade Headquarters marched from BONN to MEDINGHOVEN. 51st Battalion Welsh Regiment marched from BONN to MECKENHEIM. 52nd Battalion Welsh Regiment marched from BONN to DUISDORF. 53rd Battalion Welsh Regiment marched from BONN to ALFTER. 2nd Western Trench Mortar Battery marched from BONN to MESSDORF. No.2 Field Ambulance marched from BONN to MESSDORF. No.3 Company Western Divisional Train marched from BONN to IPSKOVEN. No.3 Section 76 Field Company R.E., rejoined its Company. "B" Company, 1st Battalion Machine Gun Corps rejoined its Battalion) leaving the Brigade 504 Battery R.F.A. rejoined the 65th Brigade Royal Field Artillery) Group.	Apx

MEDINGHOVEN - 3rd July, 1919.

[signature]
Lieut. Colonel,
Commanding 2nd Western Infantry Brigade.

C O N F I D E N T I A L.

W A R   D I A R Y

of

2nd WESTERN INFANTRY BRIGADE HEADQUARTERS.

FROM 1st July, 1919.   —   TO 31st July, 1919.

--------oOo--------

[signature]

                                                                      Lieut: Colonel,
3rd August 1919.   Commanding 2nd Western Infantry Brigade.

Army Form C. 2118.

WAR DIARY

2nd Western Infantry Brigade.

~~INTELLIGENCE SUMMARY~~

JULY, 1919.

(Erase heading not required.)

Instructions regarding War Diaries and Intelligence Summaries are contained in F. S. Regs., Part II. and the Staff Manual respectively. Title pages will be prepared in manuscript.

Place	Date	Hour	Summary of Events and Information	Remarks and references to Appendices
MED INGHOVEN	JULY 7th		2nd Western Trench Mortar Battery moved from MESSDORF to VOLMERSHOVEN.	
	8th		Bt. Major G.E.Wingfield-Stratford,/Brigade Major, proceeded to England on 1 month's leave. M.C.;	
			Captain G.B.Bruce,M.C., Staff Captain, 2nd Western Infantry Brigade, took over duties of Acting Brigade Major.	
	12th		Major M.H.Merry, M.C., 51st Welsh Regiment, took over duties of Acting Staff Captain.	
	19th		2nd Western Infantry Brigade Athletic Sports held at ALFTER.	
	26th		Two Companies ("A" and "B") 53rd Battalion Welsh Regiment, commence firing the General Musketry Course.	
	30th		Major General T.O.Marden, C.B., C.M.G., resumed command of the Brigade.	
			Brigade Boxing Tournament held at DUISDORF.	

3rd August, 1919.

[signature]

Lieut: Colonel,
Commanding 2nd Western Infantry Brigade.